BRIGHT SHENG

A NIGHT AT THE CHINESE OPERA

FOR VIOLIN AND PIANO

violin part edited by Cho-Liang Lin

ED 4374
First Printing: December 2008

ISBN: 978-1-4234-3333-0

G. SCHIRMER, Inc.

DISTRIBUTED BY

HAL•LEONARD®
CORPORATION
7777 W. BLUEMOUND RD. P.O. BOX 13819 MILWAUKEE, WI 53213

Note

A *Night at the Chinese Opera* was commissioned
by the International Violin Competition of
Indianapolis for the 2006 Competition, was
underwritten by the Christel DeHaan Family
Foundation, and dedicated to the children of
Christel House around the world.

The basic materials in this work are derived from
an instrumental interlude of the well-known
Peking Opera, *Farewell My Concubine.* In the opera,
Princess Yü bids farewell to General Xiang—her
lover and master—with a sword dance before she
kills herself at the climactic point of the dance.
Here I imagine the violin part delivers the female
singing voice as well as the Peking Opera fiddle,
while the piano part often gives the rhythm of the
Chinese opera. Nonetheless, the feeling of dance
should be prevalent.

—Bright Sheng

duration ca. 10 minutes

Information on Bright Sheng and his works is available at www.schirmer.com

A NIGHT AT THE CHINESE OPERA

Bright Sheng

* Silently depress all keys between and including A and E, holding with the sostenuto pedal until the downbeat of m. 45.

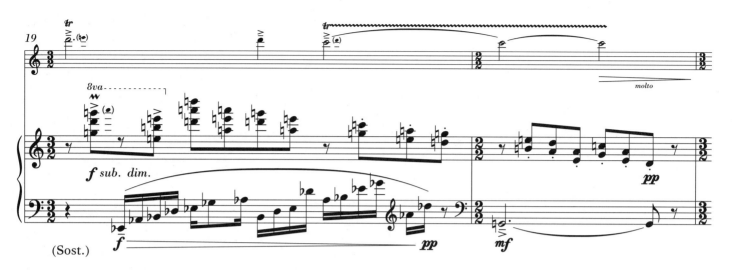

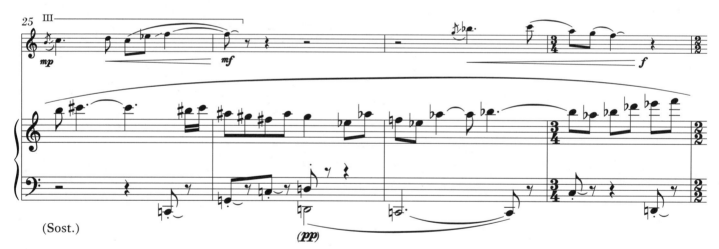

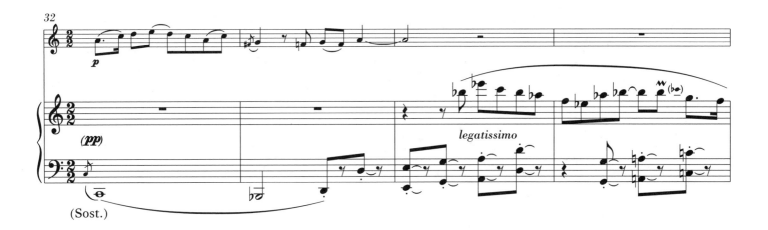

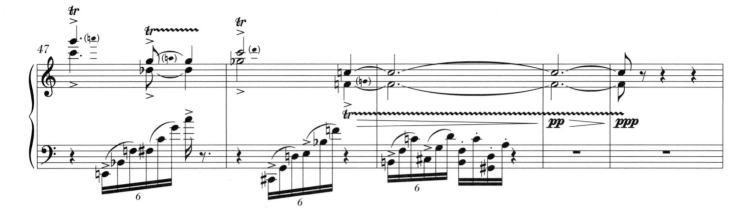

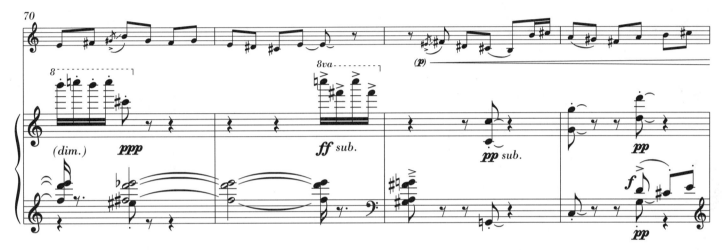

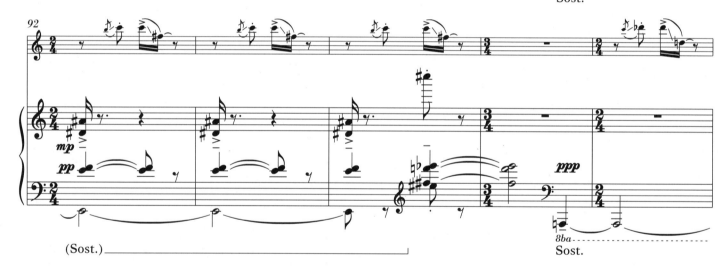

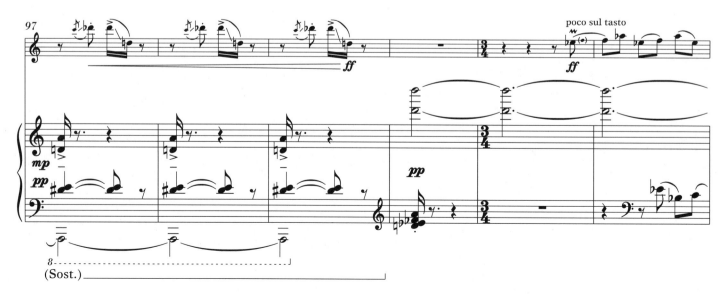

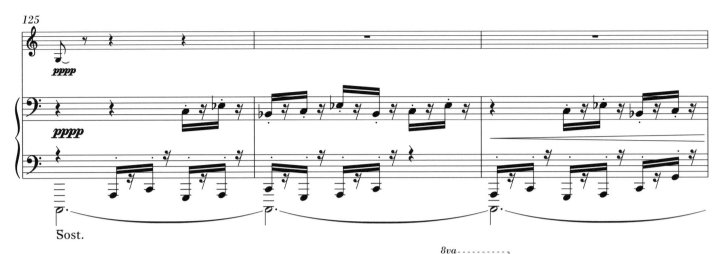

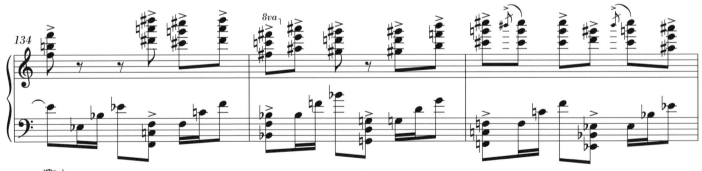

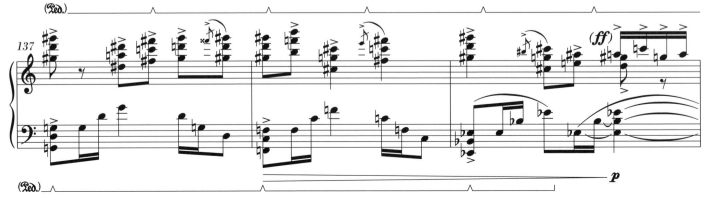

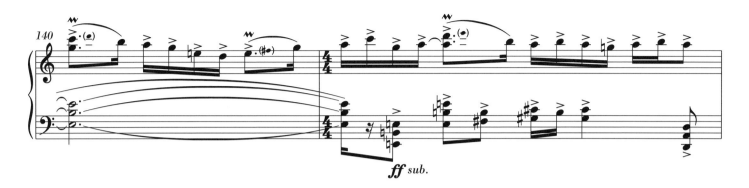

* "x" note heads indicate approximate pitches

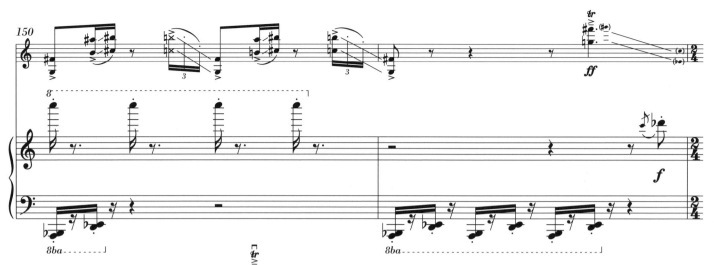

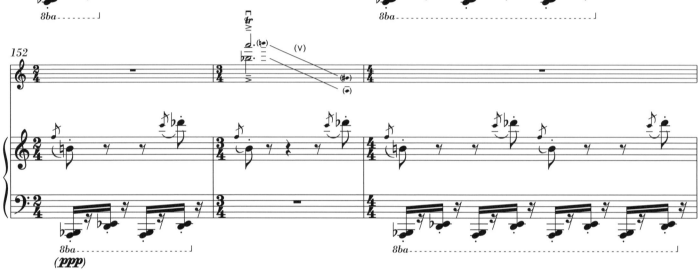

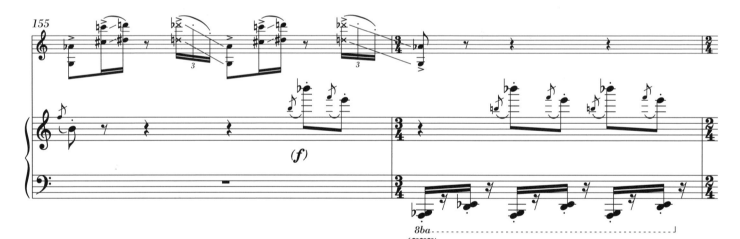

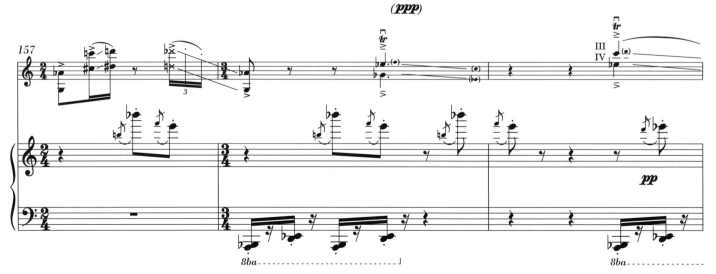

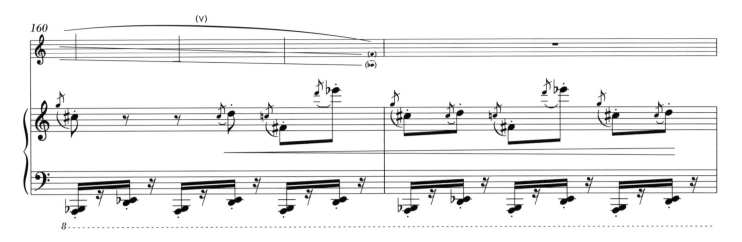

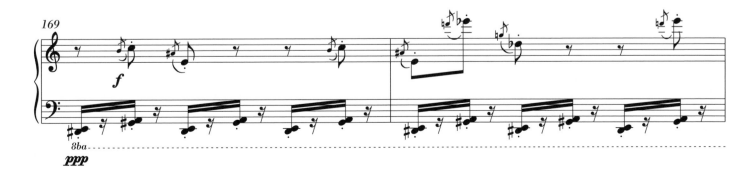

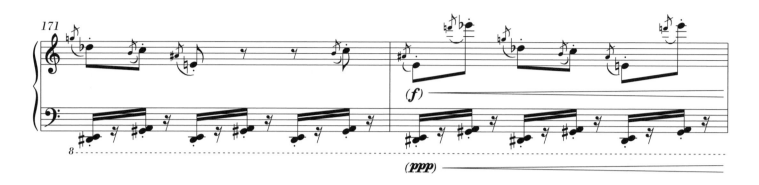

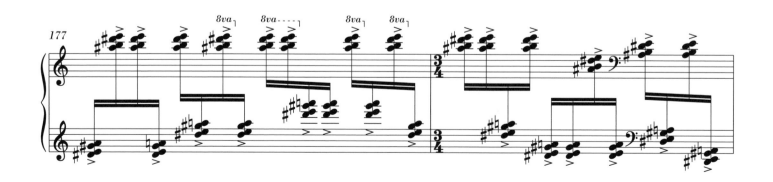

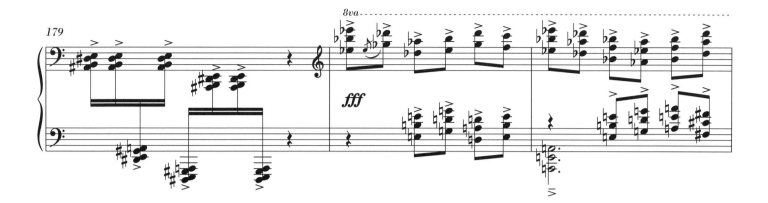

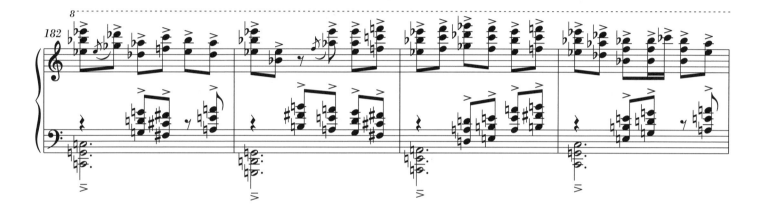

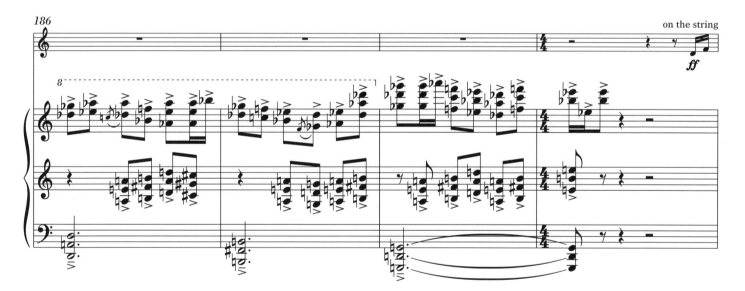

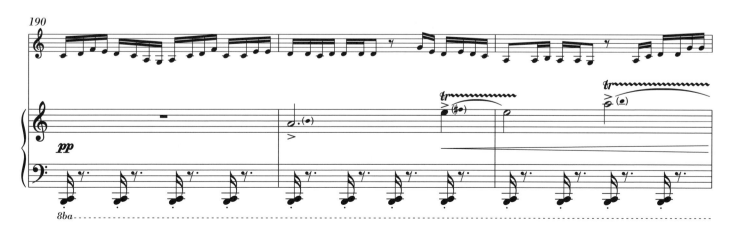

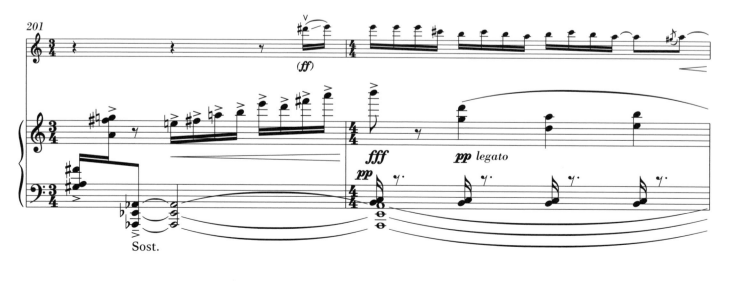

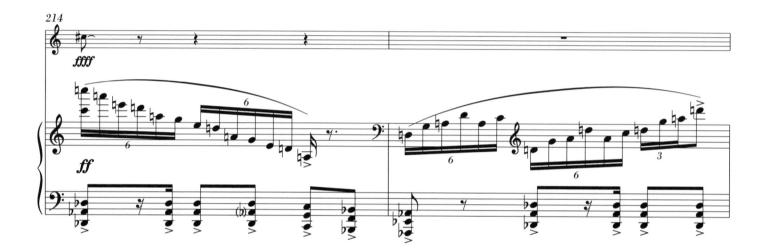

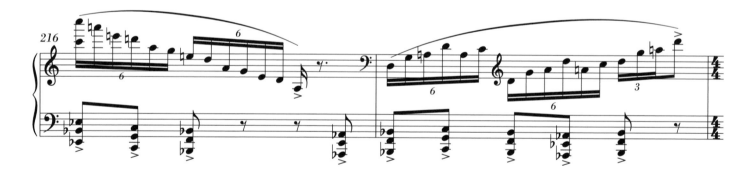

BRIGHT SHENG

A NIGHT AT THE CHINESE OPERA

FOR VIOLIN AND PIANO
edited by Cho-Liang Lin

Violin

ED 4374
First Printing: December 2008

ISBN: 978-1-4234-3333-0

G. SCHIRMER, Inc.

DISTRIBUTED BY

HAL•LEONARD®
CORPORATION

7777 W. BLUEMOUND RD. P.O. BOX 13819 MILWAUKEE, WI 53213

A NIGHT AT THE CHINESE OPERA

Violin

Bright Sheng

edited by Cho-Liang Lin

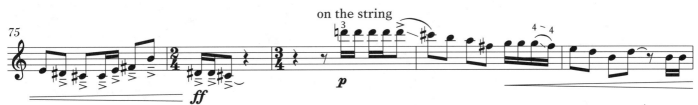

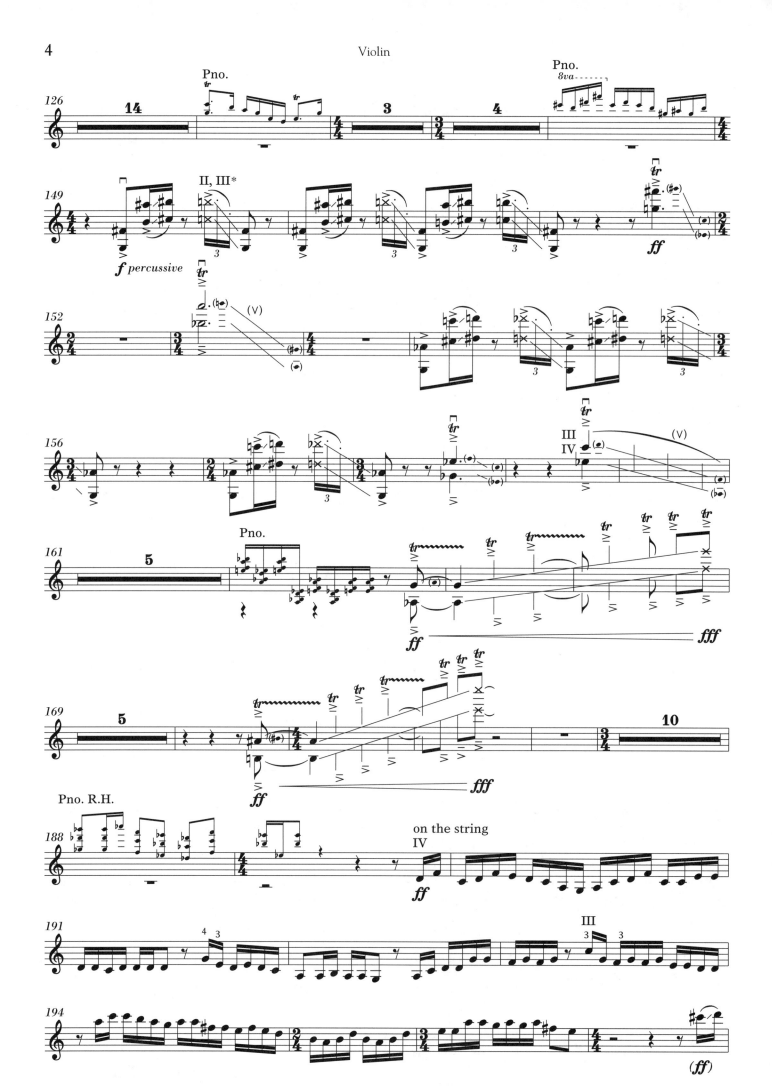

* "x" note heads indicate approximate pitches

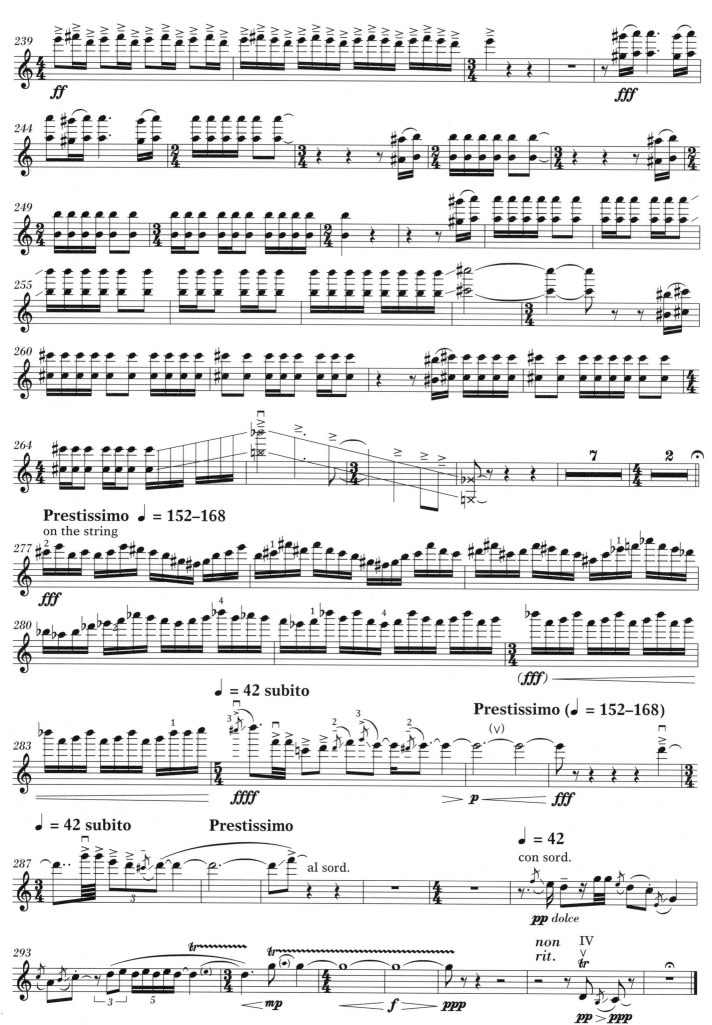

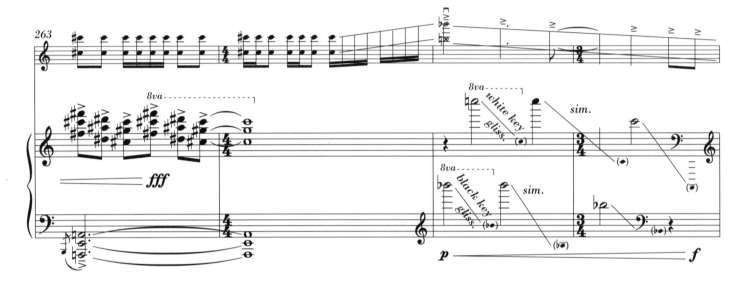

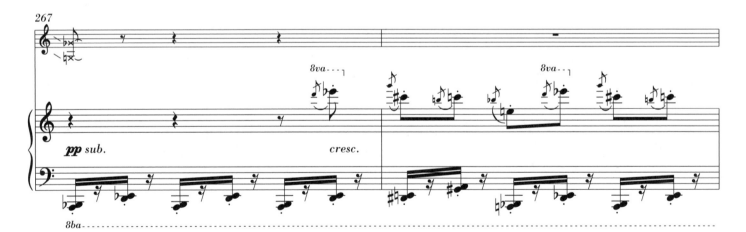

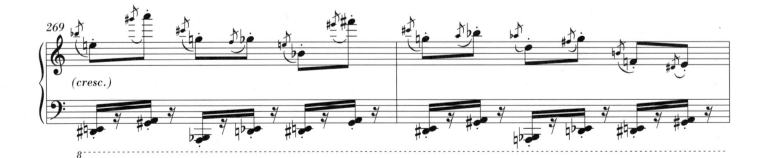

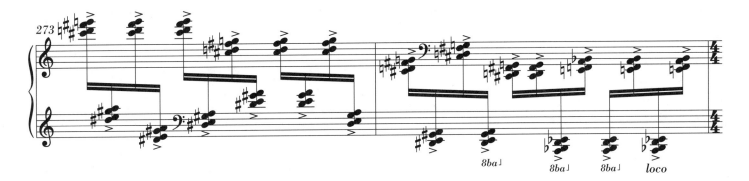

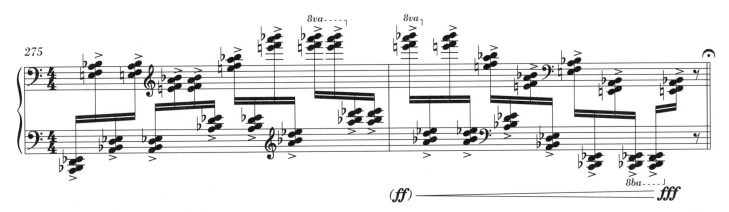

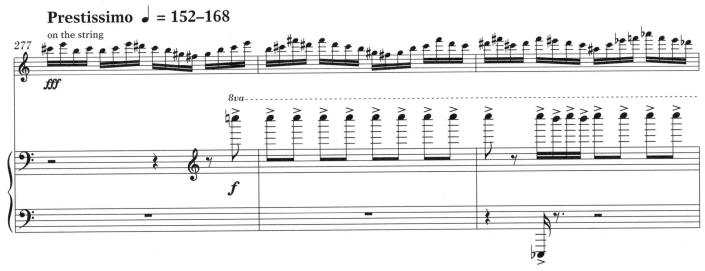

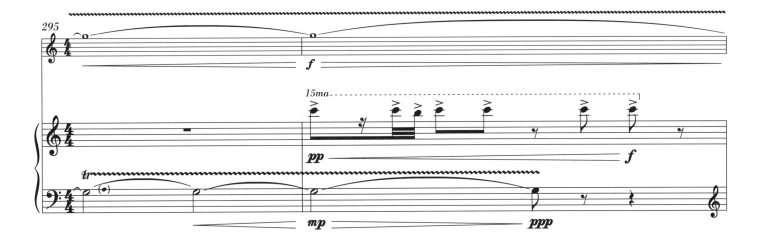

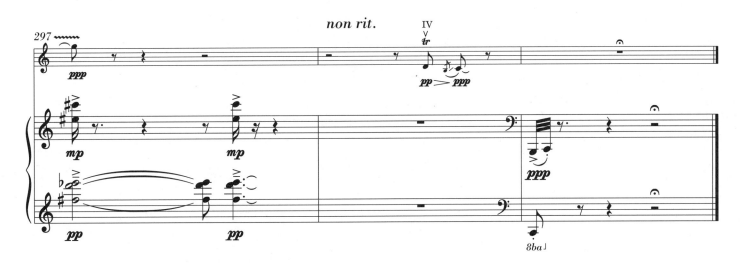